AF362048

DEDICATION

This book is dedicated to every aspiring African Female who is pushing the boundaries of where they are, and aiming to do more or be more.

All dreams are possible. Ellen did it so we can too!

Keep going, you are a rare diamond in our world.

- OVO

<u>AUTHOR'S INTERESTING COMMENT</u>

As a West African, I have always admired the Liberian culture, food and dressing, but I have neither been to Liberia nor met the amazing former female president - Ellen.

One day when I do visit Liberia and hopefully have the rare privilege of meeting Ellen, I know I will ask her one zillion questions all at once…..

I just hope she will be able to answer ALL.

Smiles…

DISCLAIMER

To tell the story of this inspiring and historic character, we have researched and written based on facts, history, and available information. Some parts of which are unfortunately unverifiable. Some parts of this book have also been written as fiction; speculated in order to make it relatable to the reader.

No part of this book may be quoted as exact events. Some parts of this book are according to newspaper articles and articles online that are not verifiable. Hence, readers should beware not to take the contents of this book as factual evidence of the exact events that happened in the character's life.

The entire point of this story is to inspire and retell the story of this inspiring character as much as possible to the reader.

Read on and be inspired.

Inspire HQ Team

This book belongs to:
____

Be inspired by

ELLEN JOHNSON SIRLEAF

WRITTEN BY OLAMIDOTUN VOTU-OBADA

ILLUSTRATED BY KIKE JOHNSON

Part of the Be Inspired by the Greatest Series
The "BIG" Series of Inspiring African People Around the World

MONROVIA
A family of six lived in a little house in Monrovia, Liberia. Carney Johnson, Martha Johnson, and the four Johnson children. One of the Johnson children was very special - her name was Ellen.

Ellen was an interesting child with a special ability.
Although she was Liberian, she could pass for a Congolese.
While most Liberians could only speak Liberian English, Ellen
could speak the king's English, Liberian English, and her native
language, Gola.

Every summer, little Ellen traveled down to the village
with her family.
The village was called Bomi County. Ellen·never felt too
far from home when she went to Bomi County on holidays.
In the village, she stayed at her grandmother's house.
Ellen spent every summer collecting water from the
stream and making new friends in the village.

Carney Johnson, Ellen's father, was a politician. He was the first native Liberian to sit in the House of Representatives.
Martha Johnson, Ellen's mother, also came from a very important German family. So, everybody knew and loved the Johnsons.

Ellen always did well in school. She was always very excited to learn new things. Ellen's favorite classes were her government and mathematics classes. Ellen went to the College of West Africa in Monrovia for high school. After six years, she graduated with a diploma in Economics and Accounting. Everybody in the Johnson family was so proud of Ellen. There was a big celebration.

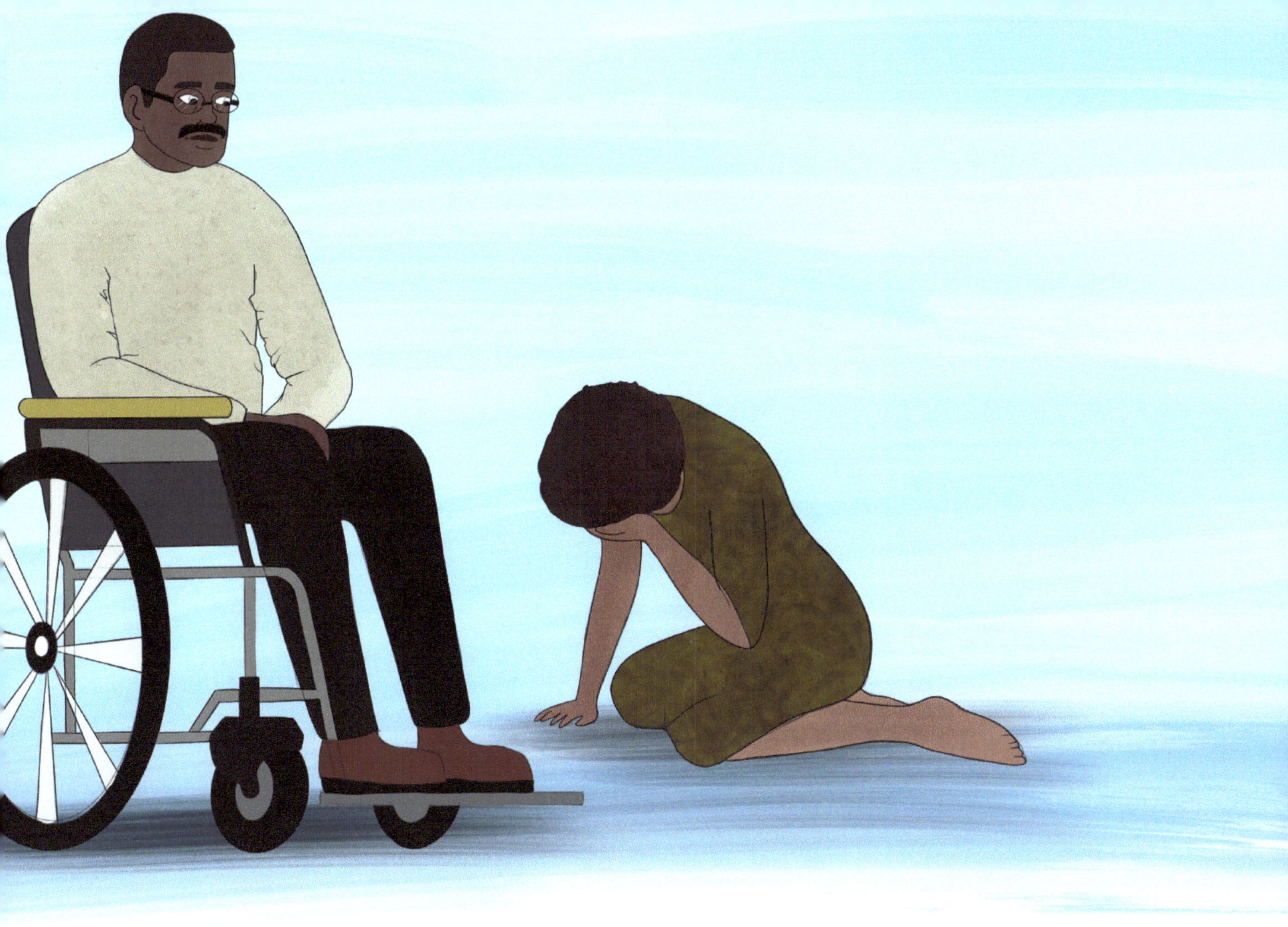

But Carney Johnson fell sick soon after. He had a stroke, and couldn't work anymore. The entire family was sad, but Ellen felt even more sad.

All her friends were traveling abroad for their education. "I will travel abroad just like my sister did. I trust my papa!" Ellen had always told her friends. Ellen never thought this would be a problem. Her father had promised to send her abroad just like her sister.

With her papa being so sick, there was so little money left
for the family to eat. Ellen had to give up on her dreams,
at least for now.

While Ellen took care of her Father, she met a handsome
young man, James Sirleaf. Everyone called him 'Doc', and
Ellen was in love with him. After her seventeenth birthday,
in 1955, Ellen got married to Doc.

DEPARTURE
ARRIVAL

Ellen and Doc lived in Doc's mother's house.
While Ellen stayed home to take care of the family,
Doc worked at the Ministry of Agriculture.

Doc and Ellen had four handsome sons; Rob,
Adamah, Charles, and Jes. Ellen loved her sons so
much and spent a lot of time caring for them.

When Ellen was 22 years old, she got the
opportunity to travel to the United States of
America for her university education.
She and her husband were going to further their
studies. They had to leave their children in the
care of their grandparents.

This was very hard for Ellen. She didn't want to
leave her children behind for four years. But she
knew they deserved a better life.

Ellen, motivated by the need to give her children a
better life, proceeded to the United States with
James Sirleaf.

In the United States, Ellen studied during the day. At night, she worked at a local store, sweeping the floor and waiting tables.

Ellen didn't like the food sold in American restaurants. But she didn't care much. She was a woman on a mission. Soon after, Ellen graduated from Madison Business College with a degree in Accounting.

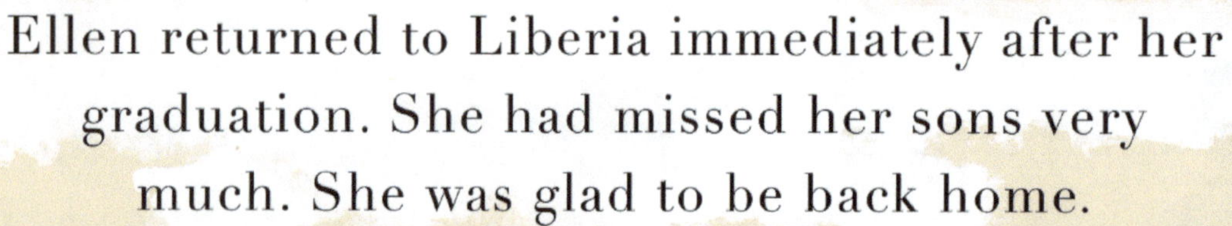

Ellen returned to Liberia immediately after her graduation. She had missed her sons very much. She was glad to be back home.

She got her first job at the Treasury Department, working as the Head of the Debt Service division. This was a very important job. Ellen was one of the first Liberian women to have such a job.

But Ellen wanted to do more for herself and her country. Once, she was invited to speak at a conference about the economy in Liberia.
Ellen prepared very carefully. This was her first big speech, and she wanted it to be remarkable. When Ellen delivered her speech, many people were not pleased.
She spoke about the bad things happening in Liberia's government offices. Liberia became unsafe for Ellen because of her speech. So, she had to leave Liberia for some time.

After getting her master's degree from Harvard, Ellen returned to Liberia. She hoped that she could now help her country become a better place. Unfortunately, the government at the time was very bad, and Ellen was not shy to say it.

Ellen got a job as the Assistant Minister of Finance. However, very few people liked Ellen at work. This was because she was always speaking against the dishonest things being done by the ruling government. Ellen did not stay on that job for long. Ellen got another job with the World Bank, working from its headquarters in the United States. This job made Ellen very happy.
At the World Bank, Ellen was a bright star. She got promoted very quickly. Ellen's boss, Alan Berg, really believed in her. And Ellen always made Alan proud.

Ellen enjoyed her time at the World Bank Headquarters. The people were friendly, and many people liked her there. She also enjoyed the cocktail parties very much. But Ellen still believed in Liberia and she hoped she could do something to make Liberia a better country one day.

A few years later, Ellen returned to her position at the Ministry of Finance in Liberia. She also kept working for the World Bank in Liberia. Ellen was very good. She worked the two jobs at the same time.

Soon enough, the President of Liberia made Ellen the Minister of Finance. Ellen was excited. But her joy did not last very long. The military took control of the government shortly after. Ellen had to return to the United States. There, she worked with the World Bank, Equator bank and Citibank, at different intervals.

Ellen returned to Monrovia in 1984 and started the
National Democratic Party of Liberia (NDPL).

Ellen continued to speak against the corruption in
Liberia. She spoke against all the dishonest things
people in government were doing.

In 1985, Ellen ran for the position of Vice-President. But it did not end well. Ellen's speeches got her in trouble. Ellen was sentenced to spend 10 years in prison for the crime called "Sedition". Ellen had not committed the crime but her speeches were used against her wrongly. She was arrested alongside university students who had been protesting and imprisoned

Many people wanted Ellen to be free. Liberians knew that Ellen was a good person. So many people came out to protest. Even Ellen's friends at the World Bank fought for her release.

Shortly after her arrest, Ellen was released. When she was released, everybody rejoiced. Ellen did not leave Liberia again. She tried to run for a seat in the Senate. The general elections were not free and fair. So, even though she won the election, Ellen refused to accept the senate seat.

Ellen wanted Liberia to be a great country. And she knew she had to play her part. In 1997, Ellen ran for president against Charles Taylor. Ellen didn't win the election. She was exiled to Ivory Coast for a while.

But Ellen wasn't going to give up yet. In 2005, Ellen ran for the President of Liberia again. This time, she won!

After so many years, Ellen became the 24th President of Liberia and the first female President in Africa.

President Ellen Sirleaf Johnson was also awarded the Nobel Prize for Peace in Liberia and fighting for women's rights.

She is indeed an inspiring icon to remember forever.

President Ellen is an inspiration to everyone all around the world.

She says, "If your dreams do not scare you, they are not big enough."

TIMELINE

1988 - Ellen receives the Roosevelt Institute Freedom of Speech Award

1996 - Ellen becomes the commander of the Order of Mono

2005 - Ellen is elected President of Liberia

2006 - Ellen becomes a Common Ground Award recipient.

2006 - Ellen receives the Laureate of the Africa Prize for Leadership for the Sustainable End of Hunger, The Hunger Project

2006 - Ellen is named Distinguished Fellow, Claus M. Halle Institute for Global Learning, Emory University

2006 - Ellen is Awarded Honorary Doctor of Laws from Marquette University

2006 - Ellen receives the David Rockefeller Bridging Leadership Award from Synergos

2007 - Ellen is awarded the Presidential Medal of Freedom, the highest civilian award given by The United States by U.S. President George W. Bush on the 5th of November 2007.

2008 - Ellen accepts the Golden Plate Award of the American Academy of Achievement

2008 - Ellen is Awarded Honorary Doctor of Laws degree from Indiana University, Dartmouth College; and Brown University.

2009 - Ellen is Awarded the EITI Award for "the rapid progress the country has made towards implementation of the EITI"

2009 - Ellen is Awarded Honorary Doctor of Humane Letters degree from the University of Tampa

2010 - Ellen is awarded Honorary Doctor of Laws degree from Yale University and Rutgers, The State University of New Jersey

2010 - The Friend of the Media in Africa Award is given to Ellen from The African Editor's Union

2011 - Ellen is Awarded Honorary Doctor of Laws degree from Harvard University

2011 - Ellen receives African Gender Award

2011 - Ellen is honored with the Nobel Peace Prize

2012 - The Indira Gandhi Prize for Peace, Disarmament and Development is given to Ellen.

2014 - Ellen is listed as the 70th most powerful woman in the world by Forbes.

2017 - In Nigeria, Ellen is awarded a title in the Nigerian chieftaincy system by Eze Samuel Ohiri of Imo, Nigeria. As a result, she is now the Ada di Ohanma of Igboland.

2018 - Ellen wins the 2017 version of the Ibrahim Prize for Achievement in African Leadership

ACCLAIMED FAMOUS SAYINGS BY ELLEN SIRLEAF JOHNSON

1. "Women work harder. And women are more honest; they have less reasons to be corrupt."
2. "I work hard, I work late, I have nothing on my conscience. When I go to bed, I sleep."
3. "As more men become more educated and women get educated, the value system has to be more enhanced and the respect for human dignity and human life is made better."
4. "I just think that unless you have that cohesiveness in the family unit, the male character tends to become very dominant, repressive and insensitive. So much of this comes also from a lack of education."
5. "Leadership is never given on a silver platter, one has to earn it."
6. "To girls and women everywhere, I issue a simple invitation. My sisters, my daughters, my friends; find your voice"
7. "We are here because we share a fundamental belief: that poverty, illiteracy, disease and inequality do not belong in the twenty-first century. We share a common purpose: to eradicate these ills for the benefit of all. And we share a common tool to achieve this: the Millennium Development Goals."
8. "The size of your dreams must always exceed your current capacity to achieve them. If your dreams do not scare you, they are not big enough."
9. "Ethnicity should enrich us; it should make us a unique people in our diversity and not be used to divide us."
10. "If your dreams do not scare you, they are not big enough."

BIBLIOGRAPHY

Here are some of the references we had fun working with to create this amazing book:

Copper, Helen. Madame President : The extraordinary journey of Ellen Johnson Sirleaf. Simon & Schuster, 2017.

Ford, Tamasin. Ellen Johnson Sirleaf: The legacy of Africa's first elected female president. BBC News, 2018.

Johnson Sirleaf, Ellen. This Child Will Be Great : Memoir of a Remarkable Life by Africa's First Woman President. Harper Perennial. 2009.

Levinson, K. Riva. Choosing the hero: my improbable journey and the rise of Africa's first woman president. Kiwai Media, Incorporated, 2016.

MacDougall, Clair. Ibrahim Prize for African Leadership Goes to Liberia's Ellen Johnson Sirleaf. The New York Times, 2018

Moore, Jina. A woman in charge: A biography of Liberia's president. The New York Times, 2017.

Mumbere, Daniel. Liberia's ex-president Sirleaf joins The Elders. African News, 2019.

Sirleaf, Amos Mohammed D. Visionary Liberia Leader : Ellen Johnson Sirleaf. Authorhouse, 2009.

Scully, Pamela. Ellen Johnson Sirleaf. Ohio University Press, 2016.

About the BIG series

Be Inspired by the Greatest series (The BIG Series)

The vision of The "BIG" Series – "Be Inspired by the Greatest" is to retell the stories of Inspiring African People beyond the boundaries of the African continent to children across the world.

Internationally, Inspire HQ writes these stories to connect our young readers to the lives of these inspiring African characters, with a vision to inspire our readers to see beyond the character, to learn from them and recreate the experiences of their lives.

At Inspire HQ, we hope every book inspires the reader to do more, be more and shine on.
Be Inspired On!

For information: www.myinspirebooks.com

Inspire HQ

ABOUT THE AUTHOR

Olamidotun is a successful entrepreneur, a best-selling children's book author, a podcast host and a prolific speaker. As a child, she read several books about great people and this motivated her to be more than she ever dreamt of. Her children's love for stories about historic people inspired her journey into writing.

In 2019, an international business publication named her on the list of 50 most inspiring women in celebration of International Women's Day. Olamidotun's books have been celebrated in schools internationally for its diversity and inclusion. She resides in North America and thrives in her roles as a successful entrepreneur, a speaker and an author.